Good vs. Evil

An Essay on the Case of Convicted Kidnapper Tammy Caison Moorer

Brenda Irish Heintzelman

pg. 1 Good vs. Evil ~ An Essay on the Case of Convicted Kidnapper Tammy Caison Moorer is an opinion essay written to explore the details of the kidnapping of 20 year-old Heather Elvis.

Good and Evil – An Essay on the Case of Convicted Kidnapper Tammy Caison Moorer is an opinion essay written to explore the details of the kidnapping of 20-year-old Heather Elvis.

Good can exist without evil,

whereas evil cannot exist without good.

--Thomas Aquinas

pg. 4 Good vs. Evil ~ An Essay on the Case of Convicted Kidnapper Tammy Caison Moorer is an opinion essay written to explore the details of the kidnapping of 20 year-old Heather Elvis.

Good vs. Evil

An Essay on the Case of Convicted Kidnapper Tammy Caison Moorer

~

pg. 6 Good vs. Evil ~ An Essay on the Case of Convicted Kidnapper Tammy Caison Moorer is an opinion essay written to explore the details of the kidnapping of 20 year-old Heather Elvis.

~

The Marriage

Tammy and Sidney Moorer got married at the Oceanside Baptist Church in 1998. Tammy was 25 and Sidney was 21 years old. The couple had three children – in 1999, in 2001, and in 2005. They home-schooled their children. Sidney worked maintaining restaurant equipment at local restaurants while Tammy says she worked part-time as a travel agent.

Sidney had a couple of minor brushes with the law including a shoplifting charge for stealing a CD and an assault charge after getting into a fight with Tammy's father.

~

The Good ~ Heather Elvis

Heather Rochelle Elvis was born on June 24, 1993 to her parents Terry and Debbie. As a young woman, Heather had an older brother and a younger sister, and by all accounts she was close to her parents and to her siblings too.

In one interview after she disappeared, her father told about her mission trip that she went on to Costa Rica in 2011. She was so excited to share her experiences with her father, not of the sightseeing or the scuba diving excursion, but most of all how she helped a woman who lived in a 10 x 10 house with a leaking roof. She said when she was done building a new roof for the woman that "The lady cried, and then I cried too".

The next day on her mission trip, Heather spent the day at the local orphanage teaching children how to read. Back at home, Heather enjoyed working with the children at her Baptist Church.

Heather graduated from St. James High School in 2011 then went on to work toward earning her Cosmetology license.

Heather was a bright eyed, energetic, beautiful young woman. She worked hard as a waitress at the Tilted Kilt in Myrtle Beach to support herself and to put herself through Cosmetology school. She was beautiful, and she enjoyed helping others to find their beauty too.

In the summer of 2013, Heather Elvis had an affair with a married man, Sidney Moorer. She met Sidney at a work-related outing and the two of them hit it off immediately. Heather was religious and she didn't feel right seeing a married man. But she was also young and easily conned by the much older man to believe that he actually loved her.

According to Heather's friend, co-worker, and roommate, Brianna, when Heather talked about Sidney she would "just sit there and blush".

When her lover's wife found out about the affair she began to stalk and torment Heather to no end. Finally, with his wife listening in on the line, Sidney told Heather they were through. He told her that she meant nothing to him. He said that she was just another woman who had spread her legs for him.

Heather was heartbroken. It would take her many weeks to realize that she had been used by her very married lover. And many more weeks still to stop beating herself up over taking part in the relationship in the first place.

She was too young to know that the lines she fell for were the same lines that scummy married guys who want to cheat on their wives use every time. And she was too naïve to realize the danger she was in or how terribly evil her ex-lover and his wife would become toward her.

She was too trusting to figure out that her life was in danger.

Heather did not call her ex-lover again. But that didn't stop his evil wife from stalking and harassing her. In the middle of it all, her co-workers, knowing how afraid she was of her ex-lover's wife, played a telephone prank on her that culminated with Heather running out the door of the restaurant she worked at long before her shift was over.

~

The Evil ~ Tammy Caison Moorer

Here is a private message that Tammy Caison Moorer sent to one of her friends on Facebook.

"Well, Sidney cheated on me in the months of September and October with a psycho whore who has since went missing and now her crazy daddy is threatening to kill my children and Sidney."

Here are text messages that Tammy sent to Heather.

"You're going to end it with my husband"

"You're going to stop talking to my husband, or else".

And most terrible of all, Tammy sent Heather photos of Tammy and Sidney having sex together. Just imagine being a 20-year-old woman who honestly believed that her lover was actually in love with her and was really leaving his wife, and then to have to see the gory photo of the middle-aged couple getting it on. Heather must have felt sick to her stomach right then and there.

Sidney would later tell the police that after his wife found out about the affair she would handcuff him to the bed so he wasn't able to sneak out of the house or to make any phone calls without her right by his side.

"When I go to sleep I am handcuffed to the bed. Tammy is the only one with the key". -Sidney Moorer

Tammy demanded that Sidney call Heather and tell her it was over between them. While Tammy listened in on the line, Sidney told Heather, "You were nothing to me. You were just someone who spread her legs".

In late October of 2013, Tammy's texts took on a more evil tone. She said, "Someone's about to get their ass beat down. Your bitch is about to take his last breath".

"You can tell me where you are right now or I will find out another way. That way won't have a great turnout for you. I'm giving you one last chance to answer before we meet in person. Only one."

This text message was soon followed by one more which read, "Hey sweetie, ready to meet the Mrs.?"

On November 1, 2013, Heather responded to her ex-lover's evil wife. She texted to Tammy, "I think you're a little obsessed with me. I'm nobody you need to worry about anymore."

On November 5, 2013, Tammy texted Heather again saying, "By the way, Dad no longer owns a phone".

Heather responded with simply a period, clearly meaning enough, we're done, leave me alone.

On November 19, 2013 the Moorer "family" left on a six-week vacation driving across country in their brand new Ford F-150 to visit Disneyland in California. They returned on December 11, 2013. And just one week later, on December 18, 2013, Heather was dropped off at home at approximately 2:00 a.m. by her date and she was never seen again by her friends or family members.

~

The Disappearance

On December 17, 2013, Heather Elvis was clearly moving on with her life. At twenty years old, Heather was working at the Tilted Kilt to support herself and to work toward earning her Cosmetology license. Heather was a beautiful young woman who had lots of friends, and a lot of fun. She had a loving family. And she had a great roommate and friend, Brianna.

Heather and Brianna worked together at the Tilted Kilt. It was a great arrangement for the two young women who would often work different shifts but would catch up on life every chance they could.

In the evening of December 17, 2013, Heather Elvis wore her favorite outfit out on her first date with a new man named Steven. This was her first time back on the dating scene after her horrific experience with the married man and his evil wife. Heather was thankful that Tammy Moorer had been leaving her alone. Or so she thought, anyway. She didn't know that Tammy Moorer was still fixated on her anger over losing total control over her husband over the summer months.

But Heather was clueless to the problems the Moorer's were having. She was living life. She had put the Moorer's behind her.

At some point between nine and ten p.m. on December 17, 2013, Heather texted her roommate Brianna a photo showing her driving her date's truck in a parking lot. She was excited to share the news that her date had just taught her how to drive a stick-shift. Heather also sent the photo to her dad with the message, "Just learned to drive stick. I'm a pro". Heather and Steven also enjoyed driving around looking at all of the Christmas lights in town.

At some point around 1:30 or 2:00 a.m. on December 18, 2014 her date, Steven, would drop Heather off at the condo she shared with Brianna. Her roommate wasn't home. She was visiting her family for the holidays. So, Heather was alone.

At 3:00 a.m. Heather called Brianna with the most horrific news. Sidney had called her and said that he missed her and that he was leaving his wife and he wanted to see Heather.

Brianna advised Heather not to make any rash decisions. She told her to get some sleep and that the two of them would talk more about it in the morning.

Heather agreed and told Brianna that she was going to surf the net for awhile and then get some sleep and she would call her when she woke up.

But for Heather, morning never came.

~

At 1:12 a.m. Sidney Moorer is caught on surveillance video in Walmart buying a home pregnancy test and a cigar.

At some point between 1:30 and 2:00 a.m. on December 18, 2013, Heather was dropped off at the condo she shared with her good friend and co-worker, Brianna, by her date, Steven. After Heather disappeared, Steven was interviewed by the police and he passed a lie-detector test.

At 1:35 a.m. there is a call made by Sidney Moorer (caught on surveillance video) from a pay phone to Heather Elvis's cell phone.

At 2:29 a.m. Heather dials the pay phone number from her cell phone and there is no answer.

At 3:00 a.m. Heather calls Brianna and tells her that Sidney had called and said he missed her and wanted to see her.

At 3:16 a.m. Heather called Sidney's cell phone. No answer.

At 3:17 a.m. Heather called Sidney's cell phone again and the call lasted four minutes and fifteen seconds.

From 3:25 a.m. until 3:37 a.m. Heather cell phone signal is traced to the boat landing known as Peach Tree Landing.

At 3:36 a.m. a dark color Ford F-150 which matches the Moorer truck to a tee is seen on surveillance video traveling in the direction from the Moorer residence to the Peach Tree Landing.

At 3:38 Heather's cell phone pings at the Peach Tree Landing.

From 3:39 to 3:40 there are two calls made from Heather's cell phone to Sidney's cell phone.

At 3:39 a.m. the Ford F-150 owned by Sidney and Tammy Moorer is seen on surveillance video approaching the Peach Tree Landing.

At 3:41 a.m. Heather's cell phone calls Sidney's cell phone.

At 3:42 a.m. Heather's cell phone is suddenly either turned off or destroyed. From this point forward, any calls to Heather's cell phone go directly to voicemail.

At 3:45 a.m. the Ford F-150 owned by Sidney and Tammy Moorer is seen on surveillance video leaving the Peach Tree Landing and heading toward the Moorer residence.

~

At her kidnapping trial, when Tammy Caison Moorer testified, she insisted that she was with Sidney when he bought the home pregnancy test and the cigar at Walmart. She said she was waiting for him in the truck and that she was talking to one of her male friends on the phone while she waited for Sidney to buy the home pregnancy test.

Tammy said that she and Sidney got home at 3:10 a.m.

At her trial, her sister Ashley testified that she was wide awake when Tammy and Sidney got home. She was living with her parents at the time, right next door to the Moorer residence. She said she sent the Moorer children home and locked the door behind them.

Tammy said that she set out to start working on her children's grades on the computer because she needed to get them turned in to the home-school organization they belonged to.

She said one of her children was awake and the other two were sleeping. And then right at 4:37 a.m. Tammy sent Sidney a text telling him to bring her some "Potlickers" and some orange juice.

Remember that for months leading up to the disappearance of Heather Elvis that Sidney and Tammy had not texted each other at all. In fact, it appears that Tammy had taken away all of her husband's freedom once she learned that he was carrying on with his mistress, including taking control of his phone.

Sidney said it himself that his wife went to work with him and basically stayed by his side all hours of the day and night. And Sidney also said that while he slept his wife handcuffed him to the bed and that she was the only person with the key.

But suddenly, it appears that Sidney was allowed some freedom, and his cell phone too.

Tammy texted for him to bring her some food.

And five years later she had the audacity to use her time on the computer and that ridiculous text for "Potlickers and orange juice" as her alibi.

She wanted to use her children as her alibi, but the court would not allow her children to testify at her trial. It seems that her children broke the rules by having their cell phones turned on and accessing the internet during their sequestration. They were not supposed to be hearing what was going on in the trial before they testified. And since they violated the rules of sequestration, the court refused to allow them to testify on their mother's behalf.

~

At dusk, the police officers knocked on Heather's parents' door. Her car had been found at the Peach Tree Landing where it is presumed that Heather was lured to by Sidney and Tammy Moorer in the wee hours of the morning on December 18, 2013.

Heather's father accompanied the police officers to Peach Tree Landing where he saw his daughter's always messy dark green Intrepid parked sideways as if Heather was in a hurry to hop right out of her car before bothering to park it correctly. Or could it be that she opened the door and was taken out of the car against her will before she had time to park it correctly?

Besides the odd way her car was parked, there were no signs of any struggle.

Heather's purse, keys, and her cell phone were missing.

~

Missing – Heather Rochelle Elvis

Last seen at 2:00 a.m. on December 18, 2013

5' tall and weighing 110 pounds, Heather has brown hair and brown eyes. Heather was said to have five tattoos at the time of her disappearance.

There was an immediate reward of $1,000 for information which quickly grew to a $10,000 reward within just a few days. Before long, the reward grew to $30,000 for any information which could lead to finding Heather or finding out what had happened to her.

There were literally thousands of anonymous tips sent in to the local police department which kept the investigators busy following up on every lead. But right from the start the investigators knew it in their gut that the Moorers were somehow responsible for the disappearance of Heather Elvis. There was just one problem. They didn't have any evidence to support their claim. Whatever the Moorer's did to Heather Elvis they surely must have planned it out and carried it out in such a way as to make finding any evidence of their involvement to be next to impossible.

But the police detectives and the prosecutors are not professionals who give up very easily. With Heather's family and friends trusting that one day justice will be done, law enforcement continued on with their investigation. And what they soon learned was finally enough to put both Sidney and Tammy Moorer behind bars.

~

The Lies

Tammy's husband, Sidney Moorer will also be tried, and presumably convicted, of kidnapping, and conspiracy to commit kidnapping, later this year. At this time, he is serving a ten-year prison term after being convicted of obstructing justice in the investigation shortly after his young mistress, Heather Elvis, disappeared. In short, he lied to the police investigators in an apparent attempt to steer them in the opposite direction away from himself and his wife.

Let that sink in. A young woman was missing. She was a young woman who he had a months-long affair with. He claimed he loved her. He claimed his marriage was through. He claimed he was leaving his wife behind because he wanted to spend the rest of his life with his mistress.

But when his mistress, or by that time, his ex-mistress since the young woman had already moved on with her life, when she came up missing, the man who professed his love for her lied to the authorities instead of telling the truth of what he knew.

At first he said he didn't know anything at all about any call from a payphone to Heather Elvis's cell phone – until of course he was told there was video footage showing that he was the person who made the call.

Did he care about the young woman he claimed to love? Did he want to help the authorities find her? Or was he only concerned about covering his, and his wife's, evil tracks.

When you listen to the audio tape from his police interview, he and his wife sound like they are feigning confusion over their schedules, their stories, and their lives. Even when the officers step out of the room, the couple continues to engage in dialogue that makes them sound like a couple of high schoolers in detention hall trying to get their stories straight about who TP'd the principal's house. They are caught, and they know it. Yet, they sit right there and lie to the officers with a tone to their voices of both arrogance and ignorance, the most dangerous combination of all.

Here is a statement made on www.youtube.com by one of the Moorer's supporters. My hunch is that it was written by Tammy Caison Moorer herself with a little help from her sister, Ashley Caison.

"12/20/13 TM & SM go to see Allen Large."

TM and SM stand for Tammy Moorer and her husband, Sidney Moorer. Allen Large is the detective who is working on the case of the missing woman, 20-year-old Heather Elvis, who disappeared in the early morning hours of 12/18/2103.

"They tell Allen everything & show him their phones."

Not exactly. For example, Sidney lies about whether he called Heather Elvis from a payphone. And those cell phones they showed the investigators had already been doctored up so they were showing only what they wanted others to see.

"Allen Large does 2 interviews. One w SM. #2 is with TM & SM. TM says she's leaving after this. SM is forced to stay by Allen Large & J Cauble. SM says he wants to leave & does not want to talk anymore. Allen and Jeff force SM to stay. He is NOT allowed to leave w TM."

This makes absolutely no sense. If Tammy and Sidney Moorer were not under arrest then they would have both been free to leave.

Furthermore, neither one of them were forced to talk. That's impossible. They chose to talk. They chose to talk and talk and talk some more as it appears they were trying to get their story out to the police investigators in order to steer the investigation in any direction but toward themselves.

They were not totally honest and up-front with the detectives. If you listen to the interview, you might agree that the two of them were sounding like they were attempting to act a bit confused by the dates and the times when in fact they had rehearsed their stories before they ever drove to the police station in the first place.

Tammy Caison Moorer claims that she was allowed to leave but that her husband wasn't allowed to leave with her. She claims he wanted a lawyer. She claims she drove away.

Did she call a lawyer? Did she do anything? Nope. For the next five hours straight, according to her own testimony, poor Sidney was abused by the big bad police officers because they wouldn't let him leave.

They made him talk. They forced him to confess that it was him after all who was caught on surveillance video calling Heather Elvis from the payphone. Right.

"Allen Large pulls SM into a room & tells him he will clear him and let him leave IF he will do one thing for him - just say he made a call on a payphone. Allen told SM everything would go away if he said this one thing."

This is what Tammy Caison Moorer says happened to her poor husband as soon as she drove away from the police station in "her" truck leaving her poor defenseless husband behind. She said at her trial that she wasn't there. But she knows what happened because this is what her husband told her had happened to him after she left.

Baloney. Just say he made a call to his mistress from a payphone? The call from the payphone to the missing woman's cell phone in the middle of the night within minutes of her disappearance? The phone call that clearly implicates Sidney and Tammy Caison Moorer in her abduction?

"SM agreed and Allen Large gave SM his word. SM did as he was asked. He was told he was cleared."

Really? Is that how it works? Here, just admit that you made a call from the payphone to the missing woman's cell phone and we'll all just look the other way instead of acknowledging how guilty that makes you look? So, let's take a closer look. According to Tammy Caison Moorer, her poor little innocent husband was simply doing the big bad police officers a huge favor. What a great guy. All he did was what the police officers asked him to do so he could get home to her.

Rubbish. Sidney Moorer told the police officers that it was him at the payphone who made the call to Heather Elvis's cell phone BECAUSE IT WAS HIM WHO MADE THE CALL.

Can't you just hear how that conversation went at the Moorer house when Sidney came running in the door? They made me do it, honey. They told me that if I admitted that I made the call from the payphone then we are in the clear. To which Tammy surely responded, well you are a total dumbass if you think we're in the clear! You've done it now, you moron! And then Sidney probably started to cook her favorite meal and to clean the house and take care of the kids hoping to just stay out of her way. She was in a foul mood, to be sure. While he was down at the police station for the last five hours admitting he was the one who called Heather Elvis from the payphone, she was dealing with the police officers who had shown up at the door to search their house and their truck.

Don't worry, honey. No matter what happened, no matter what you did, I'll protect you. This is all my fault. If I would have never slept with her then you would have never done what you did. Leave it to me. I'll take care of this.

"After 5 or so hours at the police station AC went to pick Sidney up. The police said to TM that SM could come home if she'd allow them to search her home, truck, & camper. She had nothing to hide so she allowed them."

"AC" is Tammy Caison Moorer's sister Ashley Caison. And like I said, my hunch is that this statement on www.youtube.com was probably written by both Tammy Caison Moorer and her sister, Ashley. Just my hunch, I know, but to include the detail that Ashley picked Sidney up at the police station makes me think that AC was happy to interject herself into the drama that was soon to unfold in her big sister's life.

My hunch was confirmed when I watched Ashley Caison testify at her sister's trial. Those women are two peas in a pod. They both have that special blend of arrogance and ignorance to their tone treating the prosecutors as if they're stupid while acting as if they are nice, kind, God-loving women while their stories change sometimes within the same sentence.

"The couple was being played and lied to and ultimately set up by HCPD. A couple of days after they told SM he was cleared they show up at the M home and take their mobile phones."

"TM asks why they were doing this after he was cleared and the office(sic) puts handcuffs on her. He tells her not to question him or she'll go to jail right now."

Right. The big mean police officers showed up to take their cell phones and poor little Tammy Caison Moorer was immediately placed in handcuffs through no fault of her own. Could it be she became verbally abusive toward the police officers? Could it be that she became combative? Why would the officers have placed her in handcuffs simply to retrieve their cell phones?

"SM tells the officer he's going to tell the chief what was done to him on 12/20/13, how he was forced to admit to something so he could leave. SM never called HE from that payphone."

If Sidney Moorer never called Heather Elvis from that payphone then why on earth was he seen on the surveillance video making that call? And if he never called anyone from that payphone then why on earth would he have admitted to it? Could it be that after learning he was caught making that call that he figured he may as well tell the truth? Or could it be that the only "truth" that Sidney Moorer knows is what his bully wife tells him it is?

"Actually at 11:21PM 12/17/13 HE texts that "payphone" number, HE texts the # and then at 1:35 that # she had texted calls her back!"

I think what the author of this little support piece for Tammy and Sidney Moorer is trying to infer is that Heather Elvis was up to no good and probably trying to connect with a drug dealer or something. However, if this claim is true, which I don't believe for one second, then surely Tammy Caison Moorer's defense team would have made sure during her kidnapping trial that the jurors would have been able to hear all about it.

"Explain this solicitor. She forgot to tell people HE texted that # first. Why? Also HE pinged by that payphone location after she began frantically calling the #. HE was doing something with that phone, some sort of business, but it was NOT with Sidney Moorer."

Well, if the prosecutor "forgot to tell people that Heather Elvis texted that phone number first" then surely Tammy's defense lawyers would have remembered. Right?

"He never used that payphone seen here in this video. Cops lie to people. Prosecutors lie to people. Phone records do not lie. They show HE texting this # at 11:21PM. Just 3 minutes before she and Stephen begin texting "after their date".

He never used that payphone? Really? Because he was caught using that payphone on surveillance video. And he admitted using that payphone to the police investigators.

"H & SS text between 11:24-11:42. The time doesn't add up to what SS told police, but this is what is on HE's phone records. Someone is not telling the truth."

That's right, "someone is not telling the truth". And that someone is Tammy Caison Moorer. SS stands for the man who Heather Elvis had started dating the night before she disappeared. His first name is Steven. And Steven passed a lie-detector test with flying colors.

"Who was HE texting at this # that night at 11:21PM on the 17th of December? Why was it so important to Allen Large that someone claim that call? Why did Allen promise Sidney he'd be cleared if he'd just agree to that one thing?"

The answer is clear – the person writing the support piece on youtube is lying. It was Sidney Moorer who made that call from the payphone. And since Tammy Caison Moorer was by her cheating husband's side 24/7, it is likely that Tammy Caison Moorer was sitting right in the truck waiting for her husband to lure Heather Elvis to a meeting with him so that she could kidnap the woman and get her out of her marriage for good.

But Heather Elvis was already out of the way. She had already moved on with her life. She was supporting herself with a good job while also studying cosmetology. She was dating a new man. She had not called Sidney Moorer at all. And when Tammy Caison Moorer was stalking her, Heather Elvis tried her best to ignore her after telling her to just leave her alone.

The Court Testimony

Just like convicted killers Jodi Arias and Darlie Routier before her, Tammy Caison took the stand to testify in her own defense at her kidnapping trial. And just like Arias and Routier, it appears from her testimony that everybody, but her of course, is lying.

If Tammy Caison Moorer thought it was a good idea for her to get up on that stand, just like Arias and Routier, she was sadly mistaken. Like her sister Ashley who testified before her, Tammy came across as an evil, dishonest, angry, and combative woman.

"I promise you that on this Holy Bible". Tammy Caison Moorer showed her true colors during cross-examination. She tried to control the situation just like she had tried to control her philandering husband. And just like trying to keep her cheating husband for herself, when she tried so hard to control the courtroom, she failed.

Big time.

She made reference to the Lord as if she was some sort of true believer who would never tell a lie. All while she sat there on the stand with a smirk on her face, glancing over toward the jurors repeatedly, as if to say, lookey there y'all, I'm making a fool of the prosecutor right now.

But she wasn't. She was making a fool of herself.

Tammy insisted that the experts who testified for the state were not experts at all. She accused the prosecutor of paying the experts to lie. She claimed that the video surveillance did not show "her" truck driving from her home directly to the Peach Tree Landing, where Heather Elvis's car was found.

Her repeated attempts to warm up to the jurors failed. Because on that witness stand, Tammy came across as cold as ice.

Cheating on your spouse is never okay. That's a given. But I have to admit that while I was watching Tammy testify during her kidnapping trial that I thought to myself "no wonder her husband had a girlfriend".

So every once in a while when Tammy would look over at the jurors and smirk as if to say Look at me, I'm so smart, I am shredding this case to bits and pieces, instead she was showing the jurors up close just how two-faced and evil she could be.

"My Ford F-150 never went to the Peach Tree Landing that night".

Except the experts said that the truck on the surveillance video was, in fact, "her" Ford F-150.

"People lie, Nancy".

When Tammy blurted out "People lie, Nancy" to the prosecutor she sunk her own ship right then and there. Evidently, she is so full of herself that she believes she's on a first-name basis with the prosecutor the same way she refers to her defense lawyer as "Greg". Tammy seemed to want to appear as if she had a law degree too when she said things like "well, that's irrelevant to this case" or "that would be hearsay, and hearsay is not allowed".

Over and over again, Tammy would flat out ignore the prosecutor's questions and take off running with whatever accusation against law enforcement or the prosecutor's office that she wanted the jurors to hear.

Prosecutor Livesay (a.k.a. "Nancy") showed the patience of a saint as she repeated her questions then stood there waiting for the defendant to stop talking. Or perhaps the prosecutor wasn't being patient at all. Maybe she was setting the trap for the talkative, and seemingly angry, defendant to fall into. Maybe the prosecutor let the defendant keep right on talking because she wanted the jurors to see the defendant in action. If she set out to have the defendant show her true colors right in front of the jurors, it worked.

If she set out for the defendant to show herself to be a liar, a cheater, an angry woman who thought the victim was "the BITCH" then her plan worked beautifully in fact because that's exactly what the defendant did.

Most glaring of all it seemed as the defendant showed the jurors what she was really made of was her need to be in total control. Through testimony it sounded like Tammy Caison Moorer demanded total control over her husband. And from her demeanor on the witness stand during her kidnapping trial, it seemed clear that Tammy Caison Moorer felt that she was the one person in control of the courtroom too.

Finally, it appeared the prosecutor grew weary of listening to the defendant's verbal gymnastics or perhaps she realized the defendant had already shown her true self to the jurors and it was time to move on.

Prosecutor - "Your Honor can we ask her to just answer my questions?"

The prosecutor's question was perfectly timed and priceless. Because what she was really saying was "Your Honor, the defendant has shown the jurors what a liar she is so can we please move forward now?"

Tammy Caison Moorer - "I don't know when those videos were made so I don't agree with you, no".

Prosecutor Livesay – "We know the videos speak for themselves".

Tammy Caison Moorer - "No, it doesn't".

Defendant - "Um, we left on the 17th, we had dinner, and we went out, yes."

Prosecutor - "You were at Broadway at the Beach?"

Defendant - "With Sidney, yes."

Prosecutor – "And you knew that Heather Elvis worked at the Tilted Kilt?".

The defendant kept trying to sound like Heather Elvis was insignificant to her. She didn't know if she knew where she worked. Oh wait. December? Yes, Sidney had told her by then. She didn't know where she lived. She was just out within a few blocks of where Heather lived and worked to enjoy a nice night out with her husband. They were bored. She isn't a beach person so there's not a lot to do in Myrtle Beach. So they decided to go sing some karaoke. She paid no mind to where her husband's mistress worked or lived.

The prosecutor then threw a fastball to the defendant.

And clearly the batter wasn't up.

Prosecutor - "Was the BITCH IN HIDING on the 17th?"

Defendant - "I don't know where she was on the 17th. That was the furthest thing from my mind".

With that one powerful question, the prosecutor gave the defendant the final nail for her coffin. And with her response to the question, the defendant pounded the nail right in.

Was the BITCH IN HIDING was a reference to a text message that Tammy Caison Moorer had sent to her sister who had gone looking for Heather Elvis then reported back that she hadn't found her.

Take a closer look at the defendant's answer. She didn't miss a beat. She knew right who the "bitch" was. She had tried in earlier testimony to sound like she had no ill will toward her husband's lover. She had tried to convince the jurors that she and her husband had an "open marriage" and that she thought that Heather Elvis was a sweet young girl. But when she was asked if the "Bitch" was in hiding, she knew damn well that the prosecutor was referring to the kidnapping victim, to her victim, Heather Elvis, because in her mind that's who Heather really was, the bitch.

And by responding the way she did to that question, she helped the jurors see that to the defendant, five years after Heather Elvis disappeared, that Heather continued to be nothing but "the Bitch" to Tammy Caison Moorer.

Defendant – "I've heard a lot of lies in this courtroom".

Yes, I bet that the defendant has heard a lot of lies in that courtroom. From her own mouth perhaps. And from her sister's mouth too.

Defendant – "Again, I've heard him say that but he's paid by you". Once again, the defendant is claiming that the experts are being paid to lie.

Defendant - "He's not right about everything, no."

Evidently, the defendant expects the jurors to listen to her and to ignore what the expert witnesses say.

And evidently, the defendant believes that the witness chair is actually her pulpit as she continued to rant ad nauseum instead of just answering the prosecutor's questions. Even when the prosecutor acknowledge that it must be hard for her, or that a particular may be a difficult one for her to have to answer, the defendant didn't miss a beat. Those big mean police officers. Those experts who don't know anything. The prosecutor who liked to pay people off. The witnesses who got up on the stand and changed their stories.

Finally, the judge had enough of the defendant's tangents.

The Judge – "Answer the question. After you answer the question then you can explain your answer. But you have to answer the question first."

"He was my friend at the time who I was talking to. He was not who I was having sex with".

The defendant infers that she had lovers too, just like her husband did, as if to make it appear that any extra-marital fun was really no big deal to either one of them. But of course, if extra-marital fun was no big deal to Tammy Caison Moorer then surely she would not have been stalking and harassing Heather Elvis leading up to the night that she abducted her and made her disappear.

"Caleb has nothing to do with the case". After the defendant said that Caleb has nothing to do with the case she actually laughed. In open court. While on the stand.

"On Sidney's phone? – Yeesss?" The defendant draws out her answer to infer that the prosecutor must just be plain stupid to have asked the question in the first place.

"The pregnancy test was really for Heather, wasn't it?" When the prosecutor asked this question it appeared to set the defendant off.

Defendant - "…and then you decided to twist it and tried to trick people. Heather had a period on December 9 and I'm pretty sure you'd know that if you looked at the evidence".

Prosecutor – "The pregnancy box was in Heather's trash can".

Defendant - "It wasn't during Sidney's trial".

Defendant - "I agree the witnesses have changed their testimony".

Defendant - "They've lied."

Prosecutor – "Were you here when the lady from the payphone showed up?"

Defendant – "Yeah".

Prosecutor – "About that payphone that made a call to Heather Elvis?"

Defendant – "Someone called Heather's phone but it's not Sidney and it's definitely not me"

Defendant – "I didn't make a phone call to Heather Elvis".

Defendant – "He was forced to tell the cops that when they held him against his will".

Defendant – "What you're trying to trick everyone into believing doesn't make any sense".

Prosecutor – "We've established that Heather received a call".

Prosecutor – "You know it was ten minutes after you bought the pregnancy test".

Defendant – "Why does that matter?"

Prosecutor – "You know it was ten minutes after you bought the pregnancy test".

Defendant – "Yes".

The defendant was very interested in complaining about how the police officers treated her husband shortly after Heather Elvis disappeared.

Defendant – "I was there, I was eye-witness to it".

There's an old saying in police work – "Listen closely and the criminals will tell you exactly what they don't want you to hear".

I believe that the defendant was there. I believe she was an eye-witness to it. But when she's saying that she was there and that she was an eye-witness to it I don't think she was really referring to how the police officers supposedly treated her husband.

I think the reason she can say those words with such force and conviction is because she was there the moment that Heather Elvis was kidnapped.

In her next breath, she admits that she really wasn't there after all when the police officers supposedly mistreated her husband. But that's what her husband told her had happened, she claimed.

The defendant continues on ranting about how five years previous to her trial the big mean police officers forced her husband to admit that it was really him who had made the call to her victim from that pay phone.

Defendant – "...pushed him up and said you're not going anywhere. Called him a few derogatory names. Held him against his will at the police station."

Defendant – "I left Sidney. I don't know all the details except for what he's told me".

Defendant – "I know he was persuaded to admit to a phone call thinking it would send him home".

The defendant speaks to the prosecutor as if they are just a couple of old friends engaged in a little friendly squabble – "Myrtle Beach is little so if you want to say that it pinged there because of an odd reason that's, that's you, that's on you".

And then the friendly squabble gets a little bit nasty as the angry control freak defendant continues on…

Defendant – "You can use it to be sinister if you choose to. I'm telling you the truth".

She is a defendant facing two serious charges including kidnapping and conspiracy to commit kidnapping. And she thinks it's a good idea to sit up on that stand and get nasty with the prosecutor right in front of the jurors?

"Everything is within a few blocks…"

Tammy Caison Moorer shifts her gaze from the prosecutor over to the jurors and continues…

"… so, no matter how they try and twist it, it's gonna look like we were at a place when we're really over here and it's all innocent she wants to make it sound sinister like we did something bad and put us in a different location."

Then Tammy shifted her gaze back to the prosecutor and said, "You have the facts and you're not telling the people what's going on here."

The prosecutor begins to ask the defendant a question about the cleaning supplies and the shotgun shell found at her home during the search.

Defendant - "There's also a trowel. Again, that's an innocent thing that you're trying to twist for people."

Defendant – "I see the items. They saw the items".

The prosecutor asks if there was a set of handcuffs.

Defendant – "We've had two or three sets, yes".

The prosecutor asks if one of the sets of handcuffs were real handcuffs like the police use.

Prosecutor – "And that set you don't know where they are?"

Defendant – "You guys may have taken them I don't know. You've took nearly everything".

The defendant got super snarky toward the prosecutor at one point when she admitted that she and her husband were in an open marriage. She followed that statement up by saying with a smirk, "And no, you don't know who I was having sex with".

Did she ever stop to think that making that kind of statement right in front of the jurors maybe just wasn't such a great idea?

She got snarky with the prosecutor about whether or not she heard Heather Elvis's voice on the phone too.

Prosecutor – Do you remember saying "I heard her speak"?

Defendant – "I told the police that I heard her say a sentence".

"Bring me some potstickers and some orange juice." This was the text that Tammy Caison Moorer sent to her husband shortly after she kidnapped Heather Elvis. She claims that they returned home at 3:10 a.m. and that she proceeded to focus on grading her children's school papers so she could get their grades turned in to their home school program. She says she was on her computer until five or six a.m.

It's interesting to note because before that text when Tammy is telling her husband to bring her some potstickers and orange juice, the couple had not texted each other for many months in a row. Why would they considering the fact that she went to work with him and was with him every moment of every day to make sure he wasn't cheating on her anymore. And then suddenly, right after Heather Elvis disappeared, she let her husband have his phone back and started to text him from the other room so he could bring her some food.

"At 4:20 Sidney could have his phone back."

The prosecutor attempted to get the defendant to say that yes, the phone records "are what they are".

Defendant – "I never got an expert to look at mine (the phone records). I wish someone would have."

Defendant – "I don't agree with the videos. I think they were either made up or it was someone else's vehicle. I don't agree with those at all."

Defendant - "I didn't go anywhere. I don't agree with anything you're saying."

Defendant – "I don't know what I'm allowed to say when you ask me the questions because I don't want to get in trouble. I'm not a trouble making person." Right. Tammy Caison Moorer, the woman who handcuffed her husband to his bed when she slept so she didn't have to worry who he was talking to or sleeping with isn't a trouble maker alright. The woman who refused to leave Heather Elvis alone long after her relationship with Tammy's husband was over isn't a trouble maker. The woman who was stalking Heather Elvis and sending unwanted texts to Heather Elvis wasn't a trouble maker. The woman who told her sister that "the bitch must be in hiding" after her sister went looking for Heather doesn't want to cause any trouble at all.

Yeah, sure.

Prosecutor – "You've talked with your attorney, correct?"

Defendant – "Here and there, yes."

Regarding the Facebook date and time stamps the prosecutor asked the defendant – "Did you know you can change the date and time to whatever you want it to be?"

Defendant – "I do not know, but you can't change the other stuff."

Defendant – "I guess you can change it. I haven't been on Facebook for over a year."

Prosecutor – "But it shows the directions on how to change it, correct?"

Defendant - "Okay."

Defendant – "I don't know how you all do that. I don't understand".

Defendant – "I would assume that you can change anything on today's world including dates and times on videos too".

Defendant – "You showed me that you have documentation that you could change it. But it's not changed".

Defendant – "It's not confusing. This is a screenshot and that's the actual documentation".

Tammy Caison Moorer wasn't confused alright. She knew that when she said she hadn't been on Facebook for over a year that she was treading out on thin ice. In fact, she had been on Facebook during the trial. And the prosecutor got her to admit that little discrepancy right in front of the jurors.

On redirect the defense lawyer asked the defendant all about the potstickers text from 4:37 a.m. the morning that Tammy Caison Moorer kidnapped Heather Elvis.

He asked her if that's how they did that – texting each other to bring in some food from the other room. She said yes but that's not exactly true considering that she and her husband had not texted each other for many months previous to the kidnapping.

When Tammy Caison Moorer returned to the defense table she looked a little bit flustered. She looked toward her lawyer for what appeared to be her need for some reassurance. He patted her on the arm and appeared to be telling her she did just fine.

But she didn't do just fine. And by the look on her face at the close of her testimony, she knew she would soon be heading to prison.

~

The Conviction

Five long years ago Heather Elvis disappeared. And for five long years her family has been waiting for justice. Initially, both Sidney and Tammy Moorer were charged with murder, kidnapping, indecent exposure, and obstruction of justice. Heather Elvis disappeared on December 18, 2013. On March 16, 2016 the murder charges and the indecent exposure charges were dropped. In June of 2016, Sidney Moorer's kidnapping trial ended in a hung jury with a reported 10 jurors voting guilty and 2 holding out for not guilty. But justice finally came for Heather Elvis's family on 8/30/2016 the jury took just one hour to deliberate the evidence in Sidney Moorer's trial for the obstruction of justice charges. He was found guilty of lying and impeding the investigation into the disappearance of Heather Elvis and he was sentenced to serve 10 years in prison. His second kidnapping trial is expected to begin in late 2018.

In November of 2017, Sidney Moorer's lawyer asked to be released from the case citing as his reason that the relationship between himself and his client had deteriorated and was no longer workable.

Perhaps if new evidence surfaces the prosecutor will reinstate the murder charges against the couple too. But in the meantime, it looks like the kidnapping charges are the best they have.

The prosecutor was able to bring justice once more to Heather Elvis's family on 10/23/2018 at 1:17 p.m. less than one day after both the state and the defense rested their cases, when Tammy Caison Moorer was found guilty on both counts - kidnapping and conspiracy to commit kidnapping.

When the verdicts were read, Heather Elvis's family was seen hugging each other while the newly convicted kidnapper Tammy Caison Moorer sat at the defense table with a look on her face as if she hadn't heard a word anybody had just said.

It didn't take long for the jurors to vote unanimously that Tammy Caison Moorer was guilty of both kidnapping and conspiracy to commit kidnapping. She sat staring stone-faced staring at the judge. The only hint that she even heard the verdicts was shown on her face when her cheeks began to blush.

At one point, she glanced over at the jurors. At another point, she looked behind her. But for the most part, she stared straight ahead, emotionless, blank, empty.

Following a short break to look over the sentencing report, court resumed for victim impact statements and for Tammy Caison Moorer to be sentenced.

The judge sentenced her to 30 years in prison for the kidnapping conviction and to 30 years in prison for the conspiracy to commit kidnapping conviction in the disappearance of Heather Elvis. The sentences are to run concurrently with no chance of parole.

The victim impact statements were heartbreaking. First Heather Elvis's mom spoke of how Tammy Caison Moorer not only took her daughter's life but she also took her life and her family members' lives too the day she kidnapped her daughter.

Then Heather's sister stepped up to the microphone and spoke of her heartache over losing her sister. She asked the judge to please sentence the defendant with the strictest sentence possible.

And he did.

There are certainly other victims in this case besides Heather and her mom and her sister. Her dad has been attacked by the Moorers who have inferred that he was somehow responsible in his daughter's disappearance. Heather had a brother too. So her entire family will continue to suffer her loss for the rest of their lives.

But there are three more victims who will suffer in their lives too because of Tammy Caison Moorer's evil actions – her three children. While she was waiting to be sentenced she was allowed to reach over and hug her children. But she didn't. She put her arm on her older son's shoulder and whispered in his ear while her daughter leaned in as if she was trying to hear what her mother was saying.

She had the permission evidently from the sheriff deputies to hold her children tight. Surely, she must have known that she would soon be on her way to prison. But as soon as she was finished whispering in her older son's ear, she turned back around and sat right back down at the defense table.

Just imagine the pain her children have suffered through. Their parents' open marriage was all over the news. Pregnancy tests, their mother's boyfriends, their father's girlfriends, their mother handcuffing their father to his bed while he slept so their mother didn't have to worry about what he was up to.

Just imagine being her children and having their parents' filthy laundry hanging right out in public for the entire world to see.

Hopefully now with both of their parents in prison they will have family members who can take them in and raise them without the drama and mayhem that has swirled around their family since the night their father's mistress was kidnapped by their mother. And hopefully when they become adults they will make much better choices than either one of their parents ever taught them to do.

~

Social Media

On social media Tammy and her husband were both convicted of murdering Heather Elvis nearly five years ago already. So, it comes as no surprise that the comment thread was full of ugly comments about Tammy Casion Moorer on 10/23/2018 when the court resumed after the jury told the bailiff they had reached a verdict.

While people on social media waited to hear the verdicts, here are some of the comments they posted on Facebook.

"Look at that, no jewelry and she told her children to be strong. She knows she's about to be convicted".

"Justice for Heather"

"Lord, guilty verdict please!"

"She brought this on herself"

The verdicts were read. The jury found her guilty of both kidnapping and conspiracy to commit kidnapping in the disappearance of Heather Elvis.

Here are a few of the comments that were posted on Facebook while viewers were watching the verdict and sentencing online.

"Give her the max"

"No tears for Tammy"

"No tears from Tammy"

"No remorse whatsoever heartless B"

"Throw the book at her!"

"That thing is a sociopath!"

"Tammy only cares for herself"

"30 years concurrent!"

"30 years!"

"NOW, she's hugging people"

"30 years y'all!"

"Bye Tammy"

"Bye-Bye"

"Great job Nancy!"

"Nancy, you are a hero!"

"Nancy laid that final puzzle piece perfectly!"

"Awesome job Nancy!"

~

About the Author

Brenda Irish Heintzelman, BA, JD is an avid writer and speaker on the issues of family violence and child abuse. Brenda is the owner of mimediator.com and serves as a mediator and arbitrator specializing in domestic relations including custody, access, and child protection.

~

Other Books Written by Brenda Irish Heintzelman and available on Kindle and Amazon.com.

Presumed Guilty (Christopher Watts)

Unbelievable (Darlie Routier)

Confession (Darlie Routier)

The Whole Truth (Darlie Routier)

Haters (Steven Avery)

Scapegoat (Terri Horman)

The Lie (Colleen McKernon)

Above the Law (Curtis Reeves)

Sacred Bond (Sabrina Limon)

Permission to Scream (Betty Broderick)

Scapegoat (Jodi Arias)

Scapegoat (Mary Winkler)

May 19, 1983 (Diane Downs)

Preview of

PERMISSION TO SCREAM

copyright@2018

The Psychosocial Abuse of Convicted Husband Killer Betty Broderick

Brenda Irish Heintzelman

Early in the morning on November 5, 1989 Betty Broderick shot and killed her abusive ex-husband, Daniel Broderick, III. She didn't intend to hurt him. She intended to kill herself right in front of him if he refused to listen to her final plea to just leave her the hell alone.

He was a powerful well-connected lawyer who tortured Betty long after their separation with incessant court filings claiming she was mentally unstable. He wouldn't let up. And Betty couldn't take it anymore. If he refused to listen to her then her only escape was to commit suicide.

When Betty had taken just two steps into his bedroom he saw her and lunged for the phone. His sudden movement scared Betty and before she knew what was happening "the gun just went off".

Five times.

Betty Broderick was a battered woman long before the syndrome became widely known. She was beaten down for nearly twenty years straight as her husband physically, sexually, emotionally, spiritually, financially, and psychologically abused her.

Betty was stuck in the freeze response survival instinct. She didn't know how to protect and defend herself from his abuse. And in 1989 she didn't have any help.

He robbed Betty of all she held dear – her children, her home, her reputation for being a good mother, her marriage, her fair share of the marital assets, and even her china and linens too.

In front of their children he called Betty a "monster" and "the beast".

While feigning concern for his safety, he taunted Betty then acted shocked when she reacted in anger.

He told people she was crazy and would soon take her own life.

He continued to push and prod Betty until finally she decided to give him what he wanted ~ her life.

But then just seconds before she planned to pull the trigger,

suddenly the gun was pointed at her abuser,

instead of herself.

Because sometimes,

battered women fight back.

~